THIS BOOK IS DEDICATED TO MY MOM, WHO HAS BEEN MY GREATEST INSPIRATION.
ALSO DAMIEN AND KASEY FOR BELIEVING IN ME,
AND THE CENTRAL PARK FIVE FOR YOUR SACRIFICE.

Farrar Straus Giroux Books for Young Readers

An imprint of Macmillan Publishing Group, LLC

120 Broadway, New York, NY 10271

Copyright © 2021 by Tyler Gordon

All rights reserved

Color separations by Embassy Graphics

Printed in the United States of America by Phoenix Color, Hagerstown, Maryland

Text co-written with Kasey Woods
Designed by Jen Keenan
Portrait of Whoopi Goldberg based on a photograph by Timothy Greenfield-Sanders

First edition, 2021

1 3 5 7 9 10 8 6 4 2

mackids.com

Library of Congress Control Number: 2021933776

ISBN 978-0-374-38966-6

Our books may be purchased in bulk for promotional, educational, or business use.
Please contact your local bookseller or the Macmillan Corporate and Premium Sales Department
at (800) 221-7945 ext. 5442 or by email at MacmillanSpecialMarkets@macmillan.com.

WE CAN

PORTRAITS OF POWER

BY TYLER GORDON

Farrar Straus Giroux
New York

DEAR READER,

When I first realized the power of my paintbrush, I was only ten years old. I told my mom about a dream I had where God said that if I didn't use my gifts, he was going to take them away from me. At first, she didn't want to pay much attention to this because I had never painted before. Eventually, after endless pestering, she allowed me to enter my school's STEAM (science, technology, engineering, arts, mathematics) competition. I painted a portrait of our principal that actually won first place. As shocked as I was to receive the top prize, I knew that it was only the beginning.

Now, four years later, I have painted over 300 portraits, and I'm just getting started.

The people in this book are icons who have changed the world in their own groundbreaking ways. When I reflect on where I want to be in the future, I think about the accomplishments of these strong, brave people, and it gives me inspiration to put my all into everything I do.

To everyone whose portrait appears in this book, thank you for being who you are. Because of what you have accomplished, kids just like me know that we can, too.

TYLER GORDON

KAMALA HARRIS

The day I made this portrait of Vice President Kamala Devi Harris, I woke up and knew that I wanted to paint outside in the fresh air, in front of the Bay Bridge. Like me, she grew up in the San Francisco Bay Area. As I painted, I thought about Vice President Harris and all that she had accomplished by being the first woman, first African American, and first South Asian American to be elected vice president of the United States. She broke the same racial and gender barriers to become the attorney general of California. I admire how Vice President Harris fights for women and kids, LGBTQIA+ rights, the environment, and criminal justice reform.

MAYA ANGELOU

Maya Angelou was a ground-breaking poet and author who, over the course of fifty years, published seven autobiographies, including *I Know Why the Caged Bird Sings*. She also wrote essays, plays, movies, and television shows. Ms. Maya was an active participant in the civil rights movement and worked alongside Rev. Dr. Martin Luther King Jr. and Malcolm X.

REV. DR. MARTIN LUTHER KING JR.

Rev. Dr. Martin Luther King Jr. is one of the most iconic public figures that I have ever painted. He was a man led by kindness who believed in guiding the civil rights movement through principles of nonviolence and civil disobedience. His methods for achieving justice for African Americans were rooted in the same philosophy that I have used when I've been confronted by bullies who have picked on me for my differences.

JOHN LEWIS

I will always remember the day I painted the portrait of Mr. John Lewis. He had just passed away, and the news was flooded with reports of his amazing work, including his role in helping to organize the 1963 March on Washington. John Lewis was a legendary civil rights activist who marched with Rev. Dr. Martin Luther King Jr. and who endured being beaten and arrested in order to stand up for his principles.

STACEY ABRAMS

Stacey Abrams is a lawyer, politician, and voting rights activist who is credited with working to bring about record-breaking voter turnout in Georgia, which ultimately helped Joe Biden win the presidency in 2020. Ms. Stacey was nominated for a Nobel Peace Prize for these efforts. I painted her portrait the morning after Georgia's historic US special election, which gave Democrats control over the Senate.

JOE BIDEN

President Joe Biden inspires me in a very personal way. Like me, President Biden has a stutter. I was often bullied at school because of this and would pour myself into my art as an outlet for my sadness and frustration. After learning that President Biden also has a stutter, I felt empowered.

BARACK OBAMA

Former President Barack Obama was the first African American president of the United States of America, and he is the inspiration to so many children like me who believe that we, too, can become anything we can dream of. One of his major accomplishments as president was the creation of the Affordable Care Act, which provided health insurance to over 20 million previously uninsured Americans. Mr. Barack was one of the few presidents who, along with his wife, raised young children in the White House—his daughters, Sasha and Malia—and the family had dogs named Bo and Sunny. He is also an author, penning four books: *Dreams from My Father*, *The Audacity of Hope*, *Of Thee I Sing*, and *A Promised Land*.

COLIN KAEPERNICK

As an NFL football player, Colin Kaepernick recognized that he had a platform and chose to use it by sitting and kneeling during the national anthem in protest of racial injustice and police brutality against African Americans and other people of color. Unfortunately, many people did not agree with his actions, and he has paid the price for his peaceful protest by losing both fans and his place on a team. Seeing Mr. Colin's commitment to expressing his views—even when doing so came at a great personal cost—has inspired me to never give up and to stand up for what is right.

NAOMI OSAKA

This number-one-ranked player by the Women's Tennis Association is also an activist who supports the Black Lives Matter movement. She has attended protests, worn Black Lives Matter masks and apparel, and refused to play in some tournaments as a way to protest police killings of Black people.

TIGER WOODS

Tiger Woods is the man, the myth, and the legend who redefined the world of golf at just fifteen years old. Mr. Tiger, widely regarded as the best golfer in history, has won the PGA Tour eighty-two times, the Masters Tournament five times, the US Open three times, and the British Open three times. Mr. Tiger helps others through efforts such as his TGR Foundation, which empowers students to pursue their passions.

SERENA WILLIAMS

Serena Williams hails from California, like me. She grew up in the city, like me. And she began her professional career young, like me. From winning more Grand Slam titles (twenty-three) than any other woman or man during the open era, to bringing home four gold medals in the Olympics, Ms. Serena has shown me that you can accomplish great things if you work hard.

MUHAMMAD ALi

Muhammad Ali was a boxing icon who was also an active participant in the social justice movement of the 1960s and '70s. He advocated for the rights of African Americans. He refused to fight in the Vietnam War, declaring himself a conscientious objector, and in doing so became a prominent figure in the anti-war movement.

KOBE BRYANT

In his twenty-year career with the Los Angeles Lakers, Kobe Bryant became known as one of the best basketball players in the history of the game. The youngest player ever drafted to the NBA at the time, Mr. Kobe won five championship rings and broke many records, including being the youngest player to score 30,000 career points. As important as stats like these are, Mr. Kobe's drive and determination are his true legacy in the wake of his untimely passing in a tragic helicopter accident.

JACKIE ROBINSON

Jackie Robinson was a baseball great who broke the color barrier as the first African American to play in Major League Baseball. His jersey number, 42, is now retired across all major league teams as a way to honor Mr. Jackie's groundbreaking career. Mr. Jackie was inducted into the Baseball Hall of Fame in 1962 and was named one of *Time* magazine's 100 most influential people of the twentieth century.

LEBRON JAMES

My mom said that when she was growing up, everybody wanted to be like Mike (Jordan). But for my generation, it is all about being like James—LeBron James, that is. So how amazing is it that at just fourteen years old, I was commissioned to paint his portrait for the cover of *Time* magazine's Athlete of the Year issue? Mr. LeBron has made a huge impact on the game of basketball. He was the youngest draft pick in the 2003 NBA Draft and the youngest player to receive the NBA Rookie of the Year Award. He was also named NBA Finals MVP and Champion in 2012. Though all his accomplishments on the court are awesome, it is what he has done off the court that makes me truly admire him. With the LeBron James Family Foundation, he has helped open a school, construct a housing complex, and is now working to build a community center/retail plaza in his hometown of Akron, Ohio. He also founded the I Promise School to help impact the lives of boys and girls that look just like me.

MARILYN MONROE

Marilyn Monroe was an actress who was idolized by her fans. Hundreds of books, films, plays, and songs have been created in her honor since her passing. Ms. Marilyn was also an open advocate for civil rights, which was regarded as very progressive in the 1950s and '60s.

THE BEATLES

Made up of singers John Lennon, Paul McCartney, George Harrison, and Ringo Starr, the Beatles is widely known as the most influential band of all time. Thanks to my mom, I grew up listening to every kind of music imaginable—including the Beatles. The Beatles hold the record for most number-one hits on the Billboard Hot 100 chart, and their millions of passionate fans created the phenomenon known as "Beatlemania."

CHADWICK BOSEMAN

Chadwick Boseman will forever be remembered as the Black Panther, the Wakandan crime fighter and king. When the movie *Black Panther* came out in 2018, the cultural impact it had on the Black community was felt far and wide. I saw *Black Panther* five times and can recite the words from beginning to end; my friends can do the same. Mr. Chadwick embodied the pride and dignity that we all felt as we watched the film.

JANET JACKSON

Janet Jackson, a member of the famous Jackson family, is a legendary R&B and pop artist. I was inspired to capture her image on canvas when I was only ten years old. I learned she was performing in my hometown, and I wanted to gift her a painting. To my surprise, Ms. Janet invited me to one of her shows; I was even able to go backstage to give her the portrait myself.

BOB MARLEY

I know many of Bob Marley's iconic songs like "One Love," "No Woman No Cry," and "Jamming." It wasn't until I learned about the power of his music and how he used it to unite people around the world, though, that I understood why so many people love him as much as they do. Mr. Bob impacted the lives of those in need by speaking up for the poor, and he was awarded the Peace Medal of the Third World from the United Nations.

LADY GAGA

Lady Gaga is a chart-topping singer and songwriter who is also known for her philanthropy and activism. An advocate for the LGBTQIA+ community, mental health awareness, and anti-bullying, Ms. Gaga inspires me to stand up for myself and love myself. Because of my stutter, I have endured a lot of bullying from my peers at school. But when I listen to songs such as "Born This Way" by Ms. Gaga, I realize that my differences make me the amazing person that I am today.

MICHELLE OBAMA

Former First Lady Michelle Obama is a graduate of both Princeton University and Harvard Law School and is a lawyer who has championed the rights of others through her work before, during, and after her time as First Lady. She worked with the nation's public school systems and various community organizations to introduce the Healthy, Hunger-Free Kids Act and the "Let's Move!" initiative to provide kids like me with healthy food options for school lunch and to battle childhood obesity through exercise. She's a native of the South Side of Chicago and is as beloved, influential, and inspirational as her husband, former President Barack Obama.

TYLER PERRY

Tyler Perry is an actor, director, producer, and screenwriter. Tyler Perry Studios is the largest film production studio in the United States, and he is the first African American to own a major film production studio. Mr. Tyler provides many opportunities for actors of color. He is also a charitable person. Mr. Tyler once sponsored sixty-five children from a Philadelphia day camp after learning that staff at a swim club had treated them poorly.

STEVE JOBS

Every person who uses an iPhone, iPod, or Apple computer should thank Steve Jobs. He cofounded Apple Inc. in 1976 and quickly transformed it into one of the largest and most lucrative telecommunications companies in the world. By the age of twenty-five, Mr. Steve's net worth was valued at $250 million, making him one of the youngest people to ever make the *Forbes* list of the nation's richest people. He was known for his sharp mind and devotion to innovation.

OPRAH WINFREY

Oprah Winfrey revolutionized the broadcasting space with her talk show and production company, and as a result, she became the first Black woman billionaire in the United States. But this isn't why I chose to paint her portrait. While I admire her as a businessperson, I am most impressed by her philanthropy. Ms. Oprah has donated millions of dollars to various charities, schools, and other organizations in America as well as Africa.

WILL SMITH

From rapping in the 1980s to helping create one of the most memorable television shows of the 1990s (*The Fresh Prince of Bel-Air*) to acting in various blockbusters (such as *The Pursuit of Happyness*) in the 2000s, Will Smith has had a long and successful career. Mr. Will is from Philadelphia, Pennsylvania, and is my favorite actor. I am inspired by him, because I want to be more than just a kid from San Jose who is a great artist. I want to pursue many different paths.

ICE CUBE

I'm a Cali kid, which means that I grew up on the music of West Coast artists, including the one and only Ice Cube. Mr. Ice Cube is more than just a rapper; he has starred in many movies such as *Boyz n the Hood* and the *Friday* franchise. Musically, he is credited as defining the sound of West Coast rap from his work on N.W.A.'s debut album, *Straight Outta Compton*, for which he wrote most of the lyrics. Mr. Ice Cube has supported many charities and causes, and he created a clothing line in support of autism awareness.

VIOLA DAVIS

Actress and producer Viola Davis is the first African American to achieve the "Triple Crown of Acting" by winning an Academy Award, an Emmy Award, and two Tony Awards. Ms. Viola is also known for her support of human rights and advocacy for equal rights for women of color. I wanted to paint Ms. Viola because she talks openly about growing up with very little, and I find that encouraging.

AMANDA GORMAN

Amanda Gorman is a poet and activist who presented her poem "The Hill We Climb" at the inauguration of President Joe Biden. Her poetry explores topics such as systematic oppression, feminism, race, and the African diaspora. She was the first person to be named as the National Youth Poet Laureate. Ms. Amanda and I have a lot in common: We both have a twin sibling, we were both born prematurely, and we both have similar speech impediments.

PRINCE

Prince was a singer and songwriter who had a major impact on the modern music industry by creating music like "Purple Rain," "When Doves Cry," and "Kiss," which people loved and still listen to today. When he died, I wanted to find a way to honor his life. I painted his portrait outside on a warm, sunny day. When I was finished, my mom told me how much he was loved and admired, which made me proud to have captured his image on canvas.

WHOOPi GOLDBERG

I love watching Whoopi Goldberg on the daytime talk show *The View*, but until recently, I didn't know that she had such a long and successful career as an actress and comedian. She is one of very few entertainers to have won an Emmy Award, a Grammy Award, an Academy Award, and a Tony Award. She is an advocate for human and LGBTQIA+ rights and has supported HIV/AIDS awareness as well.

ANDY WARHOL

Andy Warhol started painting at an early age; like me, he painted popular celebrities; and like me, he had to cope with a neurological disorder as a child that made it difficult for him to fit in with his peers. Mr. Andy used bright colors when he painted, and early in his career, he provided illustrations for fashion magazines. He became famous for his portraits, prints, and his conception of pop art—especially his painting of Campbell's soup cans.

JIMI HENDRIX

Jimi Hendrix began playing the guitar at the age of fifteen and overcame poverty and the effects of racism to be known as the most influential electric guitarist in music history. Mr. Jimi passed away in 1970, when he was only twenty-seven years old, but he was posthumously inducted into the Rock and Roll Hall of Fame in 1992. Mr. Jimi revolutionized rock-and-roll music by popularizing various musical styles, including the sounds caused by a guitar amplifier feedback.

JEAN-MICHEL BASQUIAT

The artist I admire the most is Jean-Michel Basquiat. Mr. Jean-Michel was an iconic visual artist in the 1970s. His art was said to be a direct critique of social injustices and a lens into the Black experience. My favorite Basquiat paintings are his self-portraits. When my work is compared to Basquiat's, I consider this the ultimate compliment.